The Worlds Greatest MOM Jokes and Observations

Andre Francis

Thank you to for purchasing the Konnectd Kids Worlds Greatest Mom Jokes and Observations.

Do you want to receive free books, and get early access to books before they are released? Then come and join the Konnectd Kids Tribe by heading over to www.konnectdkids.com and clicking on the 'FREE" menu.

If you and your kids enjoyed this book, we would love for you to leave a review on Amazon. You can do this by going to the below link.

www.konnectdkids.com/review

If you are not satisfied with this book, then drop us an email at beawesome@konnectdkids.com and we will sort the problem.

Copyright

Copyright © 2021 by KONNECTD KIDS
All rights reserved. This book or any portion thereof
may not be reproduced or used in any manner whatsoever
without the express written permission of the publisher.
First Available, 2021

KONNECTD KIDS
KONNECTD SUPPLY
Supply Mechanix LLC
30 N Gould St STE R
Sheridan, Wyoming, 82801
United States of America
www.konnectdkids.com
www.konnectdsupply.com
beawesome@konnectdkids.com

Facebook.com/konnectdkids
Instagram.com/konnectdkids

FREE COLORING BOOK

Get our Konnectd Kids coloring book filled with a variety of over 100 exciting coloring images for kids of all ages.

All you have to do is **scan the code above** with your smartphone camera or enter the link below in your Internet browser to claim your offer!

https://neon.ly/freebook

Visit us at
www.konnectdkids.com

Our Products
www.etsy.com/shop/konnectd
konnectd.redbubble.com

Our Books
www.konnectdkids.com/books
www.konnectdsupply.com

Find us on Instagram
@Konnectdkids

Follow us on Facebook
facebook.com/Konnectdkids

INTRODUCTION

Mom, the glue that keeps a family together, the one who gets more requests than Uber, the person who makes things better when you are hurt, sick or upset, and most of all the one that can make things better with a bit of humor.

Dads always think they are the funny ones, but the fact of the matter is that moms are just as hilarious and have no problem laughing at themselves and the crazy situations they get into. Mom jokes are fun for the whole family.

While Dad jokes are more about puns and one-liners, Mom jokes are a little bit more cleaver and poke fun at themselves and the funny things that kids say and do while growing up.

My own mother use to think she was so funny with the little notes left in my lunch box as a kid with a funny joke.

"Why are Principals so Friendly?
Because they are Princi-PALS....
ha ha Love Mom"

Even now as an adult my Mom will come out with a funny observation (She has lots being a School Teacher) to make me chuckle and to make my day.

Where would we be without our Mom's in our lives! To honor mothers and their fantastic sense of humor I have created and compiled this book of great Mom Jokes for Mom, Dad and the whole family to enjoy.

Its time for Dad to step aside and the enjoy these great Jokes by Mom

Mom Observations

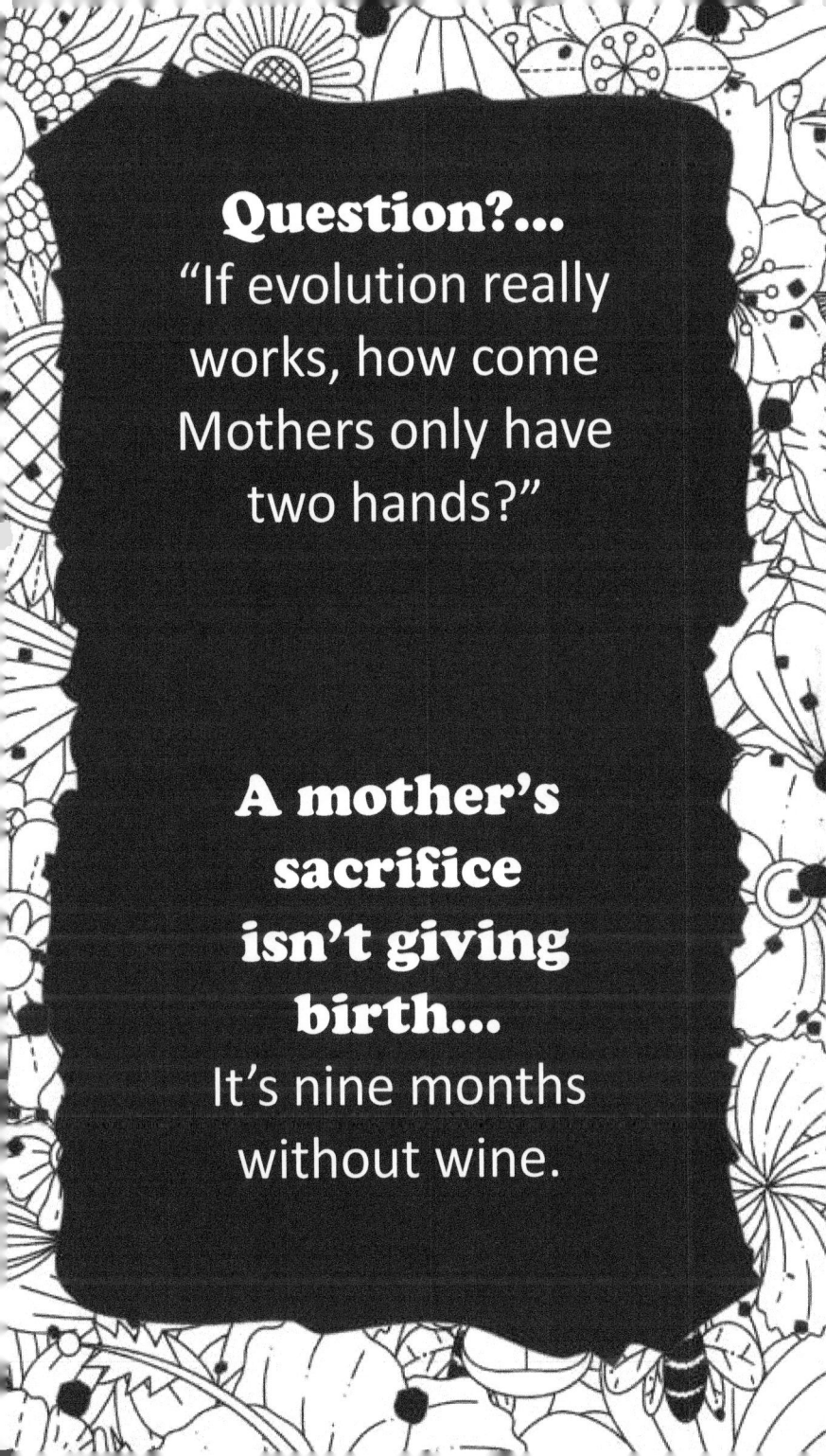

Question?...
"If evolution really works, how come Mothers only have two hands?"

A mother's sacrifice isn't giving birth...
It's nine months without wine.

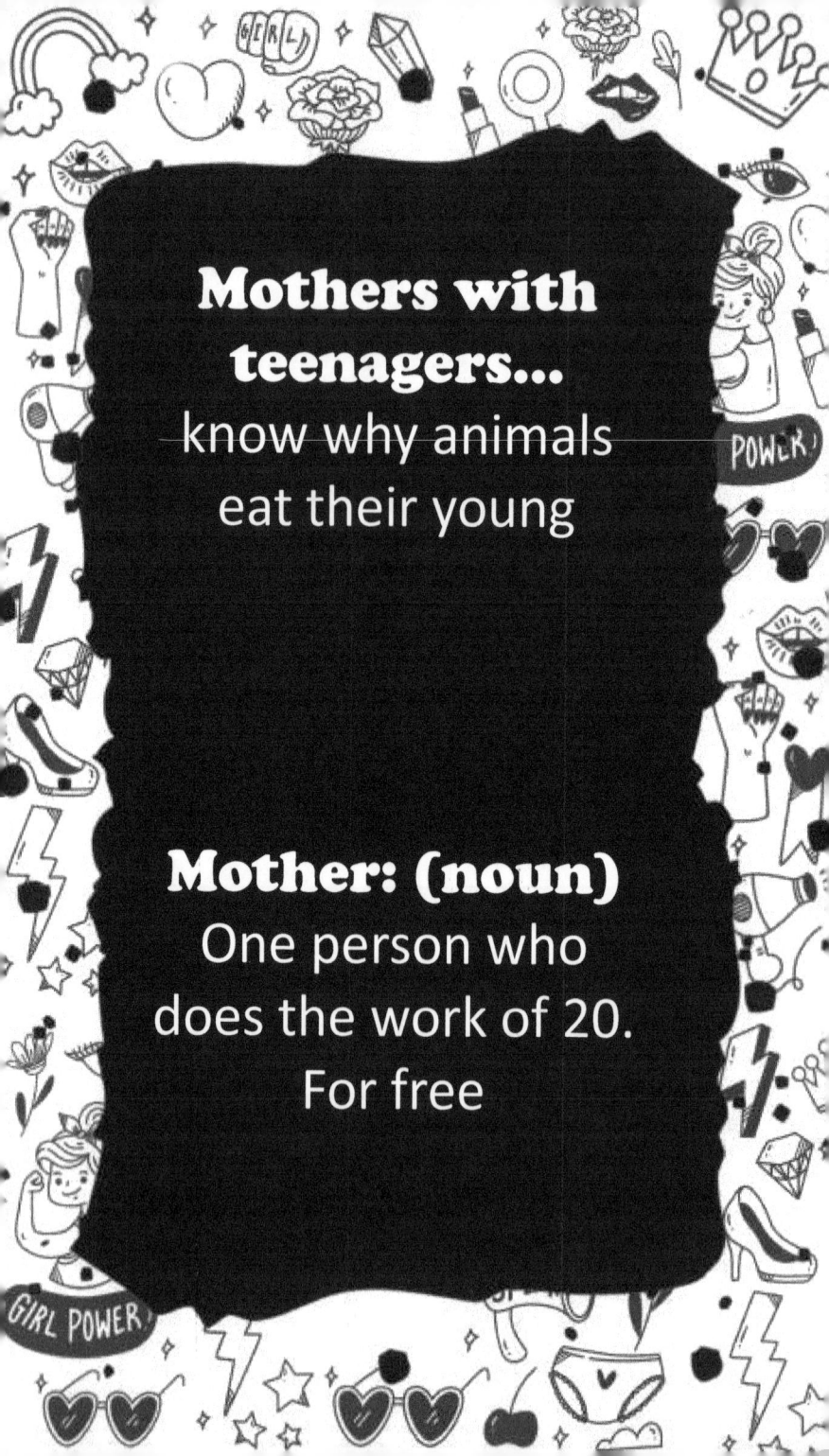

At my age I'm no longer a snack;
I'm a Happy Meal.
I come with toys and kids.

Daughter: Mom, what's it like to have the greatest daughter in the world?
Mum: I don't know dear, you'd have to ask Grandma.

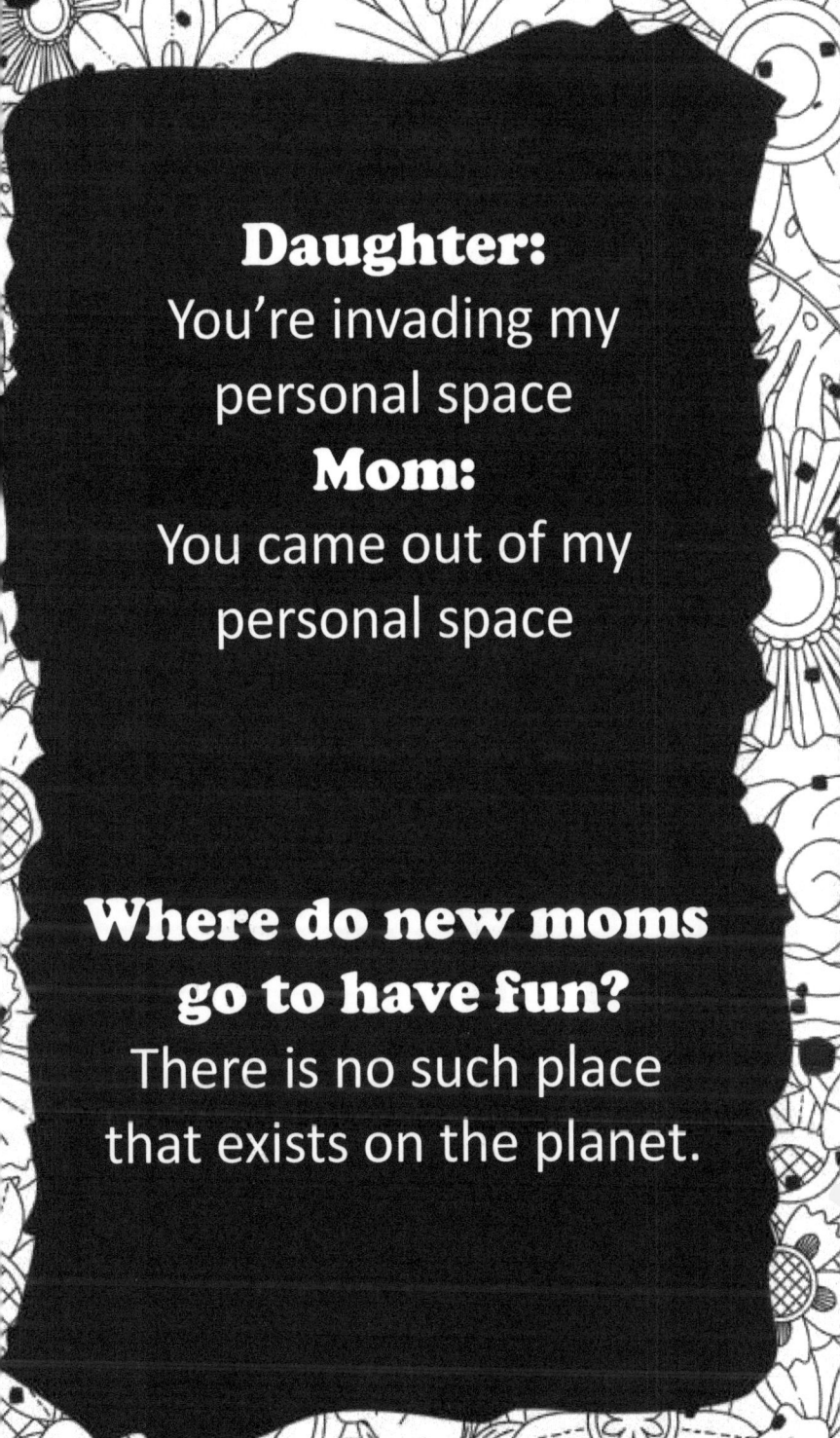

My nickname is Mom.
But my full name is
"Mom Mom Mom Mom Mom."

Motherhood is fun and all...
but have you ever had the house alone on a Saturday?

What kind of boat is barely staying afloat, yet somehow manages to function?

The mother ship

Definition: *Jumper* – something you make the kids wear when you get cold.

Two children ordered their mother to stay in bed one Mother's Day morning. As she lay there looking forward to breakfast in bed, the smell of bacon floated up from the kitchen. But after a good long wait she finally went downstairs to investigate. She found them both sitting at the table eating bacon and eggs. "As a surprise for Mother's Day," one explained, "We decided to cook our own breakfast."

Why is it that all kids think that **M.O.M** stands for Made of Money!

You know you're a mom when picking up another human to smell their butt isn't only normal, but necessary.

You know you're a mom when you understand why Mama Bear's porridge was too cold.

I hate when I'm waiting for mom to cook dinner, and then I remember I am the mom, and I have to cook dinner.

What do a new mom and a captured terrorist have in common?
The sleep deprivation is about the same.

What do new moms eat? Anything they can shove into their mouths at 2 a.m.; lots of avocados.

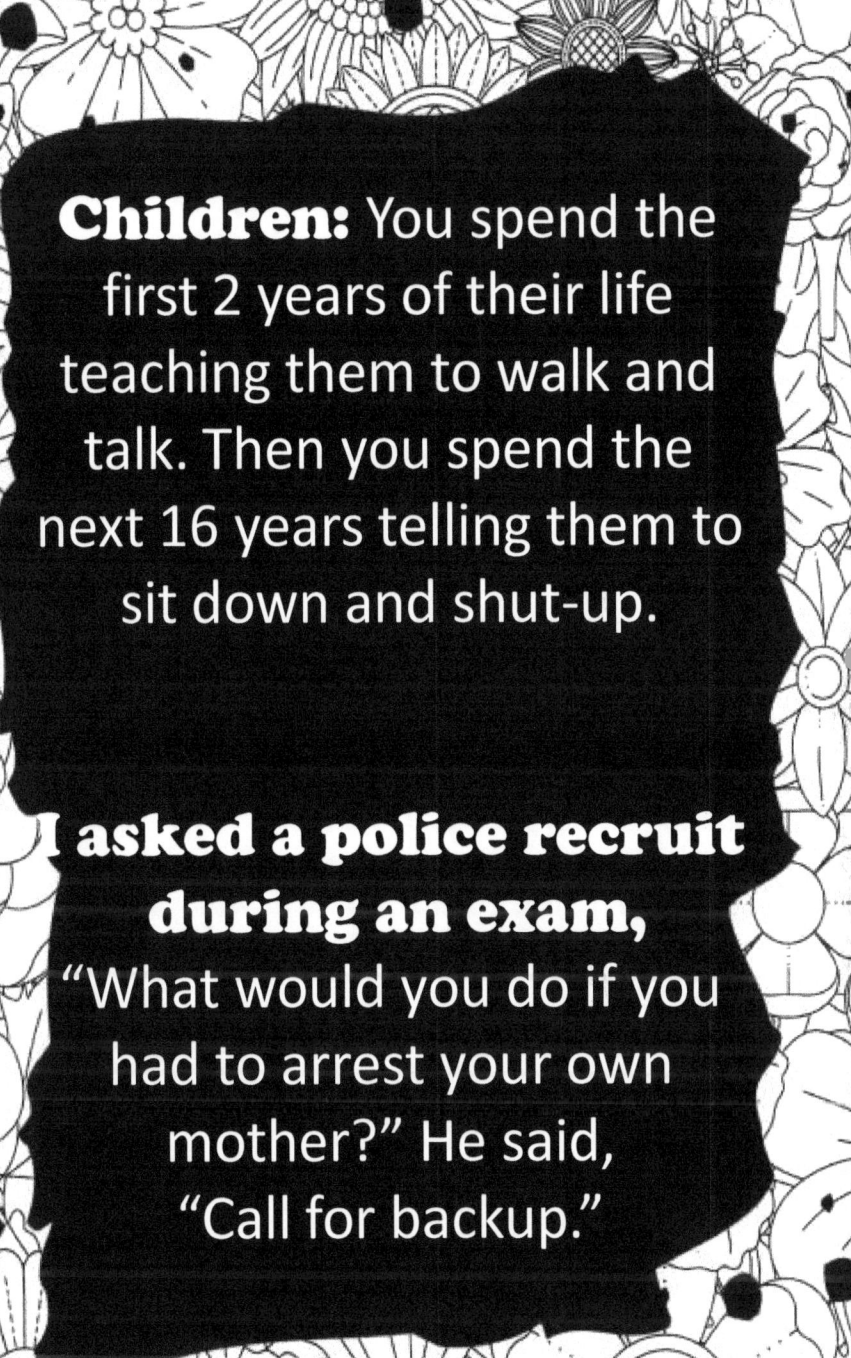

Children: You spend the first 2 years of their life teaching them to walk and talk. Then you spend the next 16 years telling them to sit down and shut-up.

I asked a police recruit during an exam, "What would you do if you had to arrest your own mother?" He said, "Call for backup."

There is a legend that if you take a shower and scream **"Mom"** three times, a nice lady appears with the towel you forgot.

Never doubt a mother! She can carry a screaming toddler, two gallons of milk, talk on her cell phone, and still slap the shit out of you for looking at her crazy.

What are the three quickest ways to spread a rumor? The internet, telephone, and *telling your mom*.

"It's spicy," is universal mom code for **"I don't want to share."**

Whoever wrote the song **"Easy Like Sunday Morning"** did not have kids.

Silence is golden. Unless you have kids, then silence is *suspicious.*

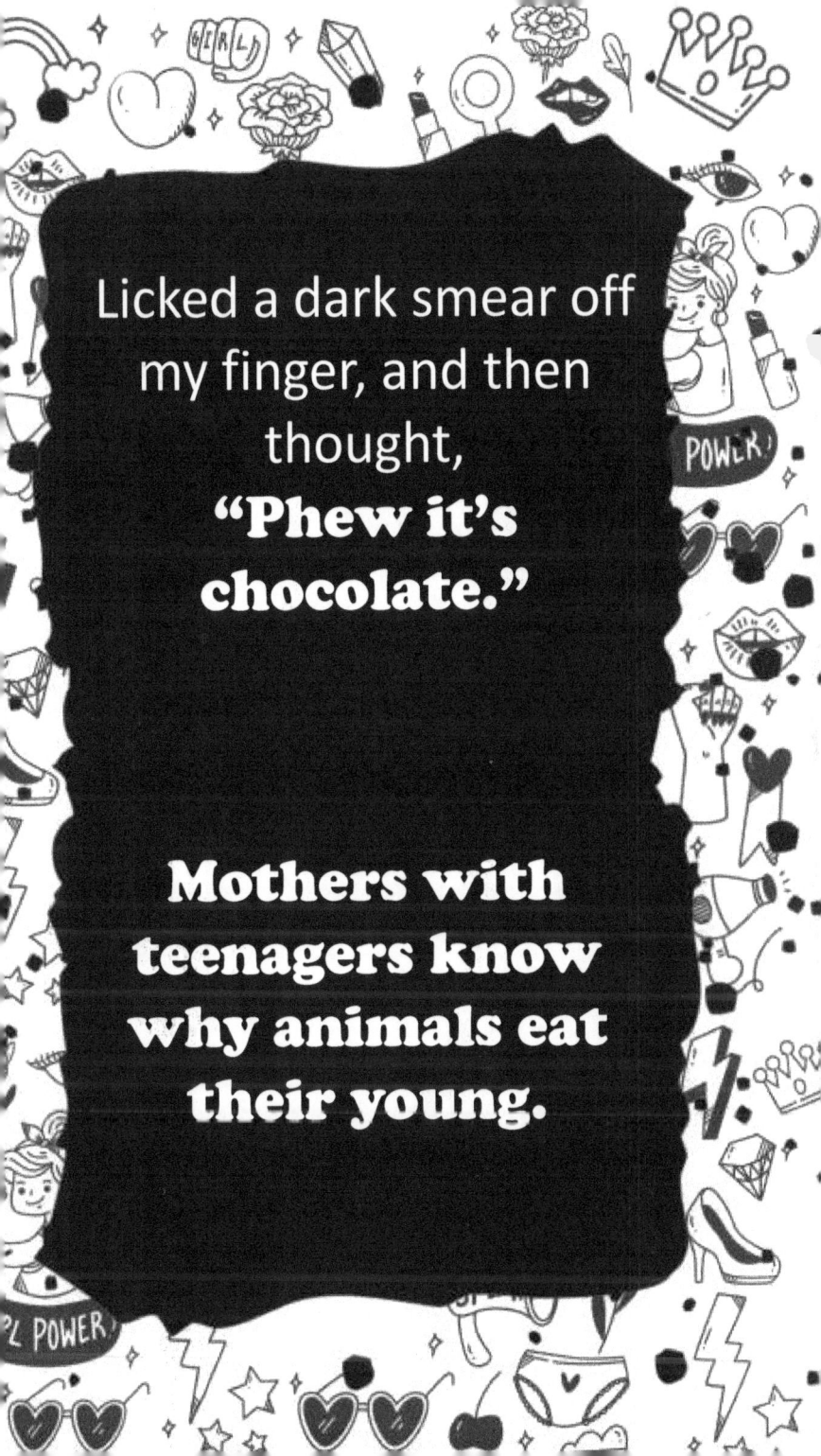

Licked a dark smear off my finger, and then thought, **"Phew it's chocolate."**

Mothers with teenagers know why animals eat their young.

I love my kids.
Not enough to flip the fish sticks halfway through cooking,
but I love them.

There are two amounts of pasta moms are good at cooking:
Not enough and enough for 3,000 people.

How many moms does it take to screw in a lightbulb?
One, obviously, and she has to do it or else it won't get done.

Finally, my winter fat is gone...
Now I have spring rolls.

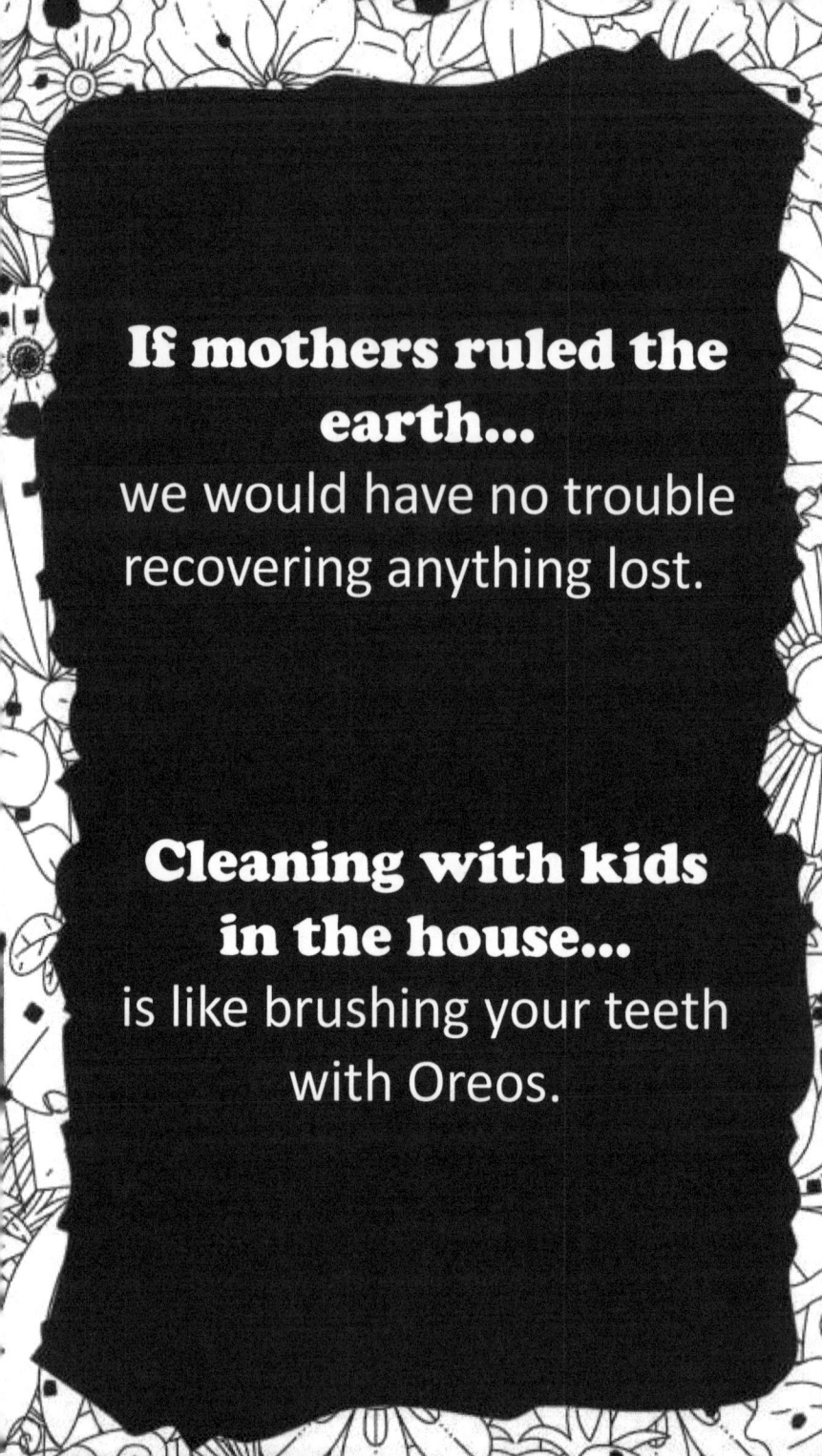

If mothers ruled the earth...
we would have no trouble recovering anything lost.

Cleaning with kids in the house...
is like brushing your teeth with Oreos.

I love it when I find myself screaming **'STOP SCREAMING'** at my kids. *That's how I teach them irony*

Why was the house so neat on Mother's Day? Because Mom spent the day before cleaning it."

They say women speak 20,000 words a day.
My daughter gets that done by breakfast."

A toddler can do more in one unsupervised minute than most people can do in a day.

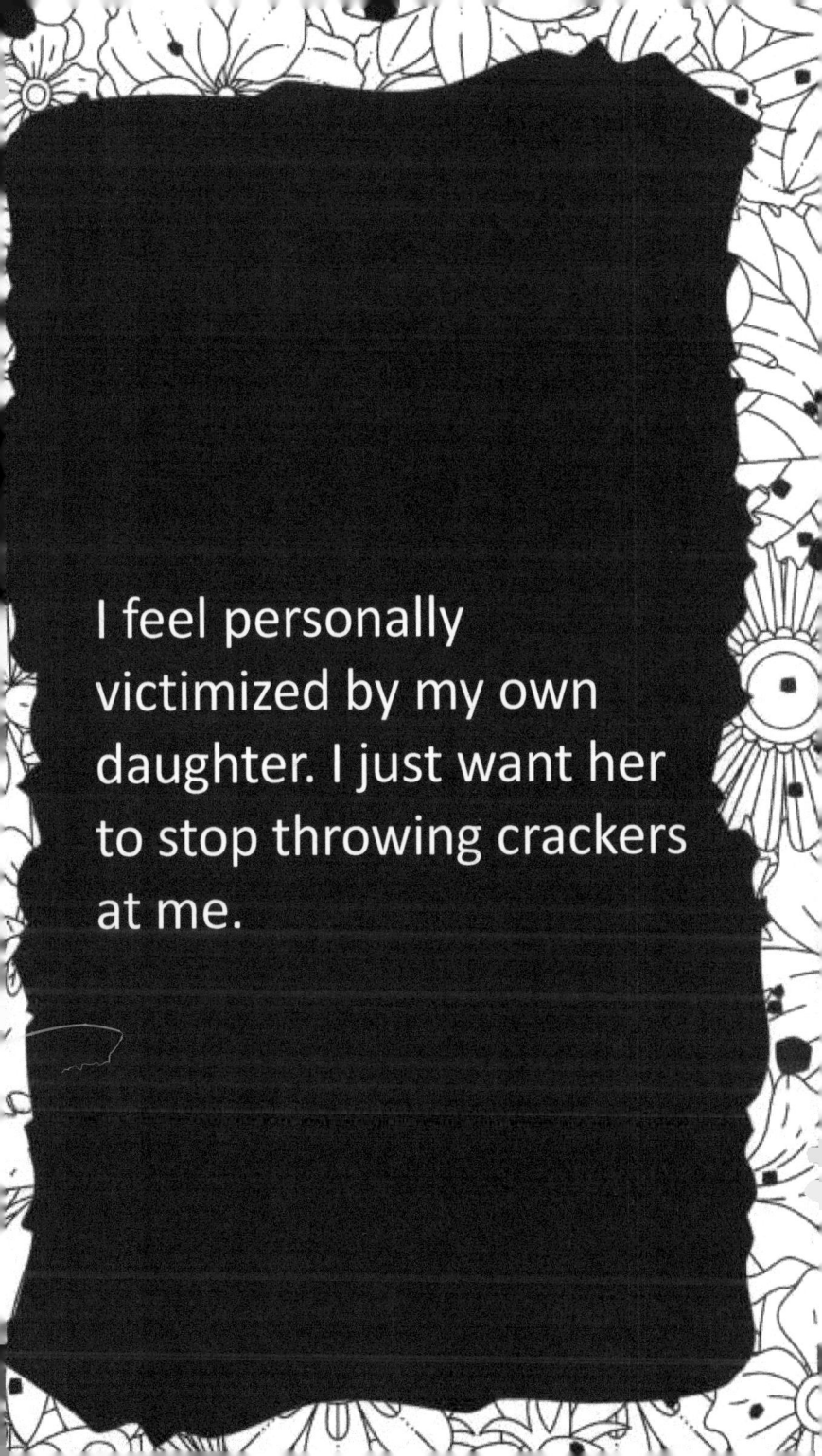

I feel personally victimized by my own daughter. I just want her to stop throwing crackers at me.

Quotes

From

MOMs

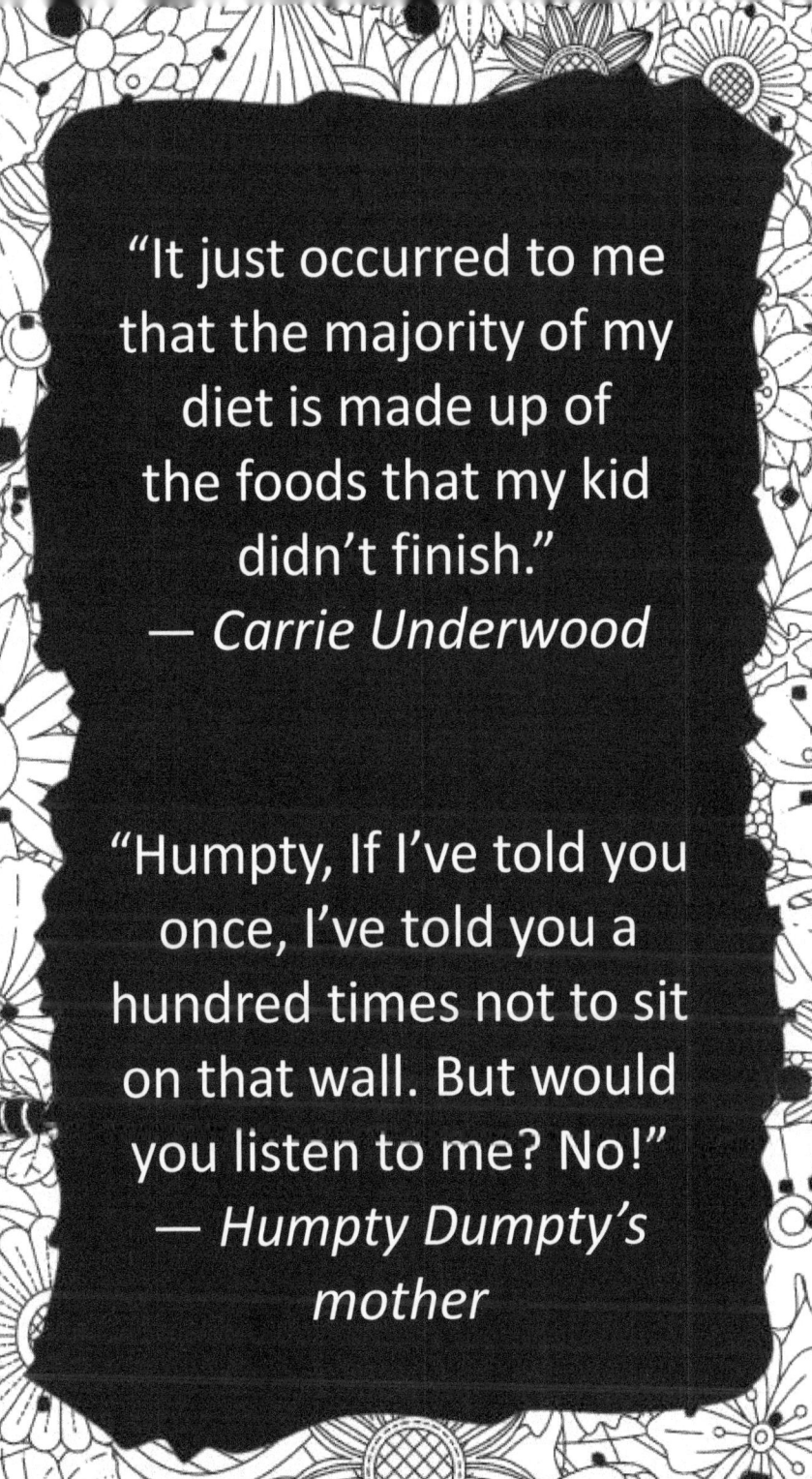

"It just occurred to me that the majority of my diet is made up of the foods that my kid didn't finish."
— *Carrie Underwood*

"Humpty, If I've told you once, I've told you a hundred times not to sit on that wall. But would you listen to me? No!"
— *Humpty Dumpty's mother*

"No one told me I would be coming home in diapers, too." — *Chrissy Teigen*

"I want my children to have all the things I couldn't afford. Then I want to move in with them." — *Phyllis Diller*

"Every day when you're raising kids, you feel like you could cry or crack up and just scream 'This is ridiculous!' because there's so much nonsense, whether it's what they're saying to you or the fact that there's avocado or poop on every surface." — *Kristen Bell*

"(Kids) are challenging. Wine is necessary. They're great though," — *Kelly Clarkson*

"How do I explain (my mom)? She is as respected as Mother Teresa, as powerful as Stalin, and as beautiful as Margaret Thatcher."
— *Leslie Knope*

"If at first you don't succeed... try doing it the way Mom told you to in the beginning."
— *Unknown*

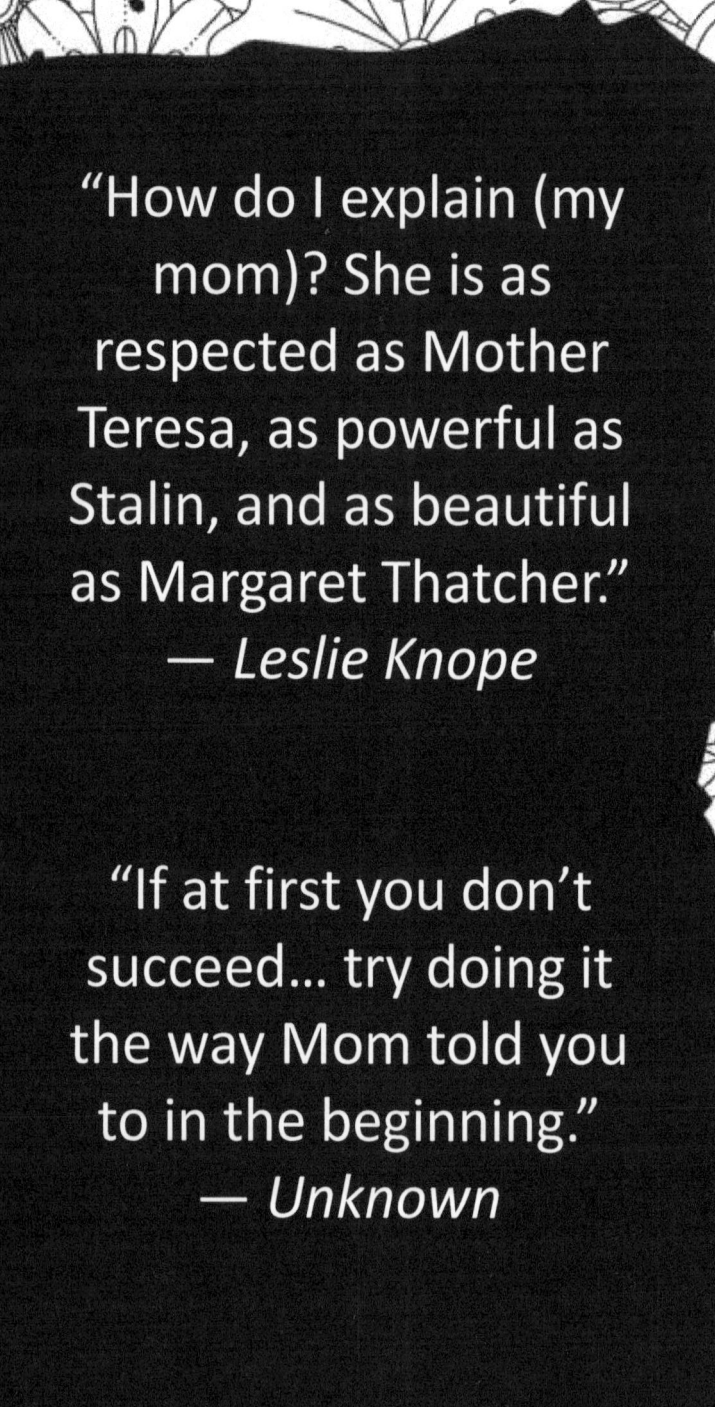

"I've got a bill here for a broken chair from the Bear family. Do you know anything about this, Goldie?"
— *Goldilocks' mother*

"I'm just a mom, standing in front of my husband, trying to say something that I can no longer remember because our kids interrupted us 175 times." — *Mommy Owl*

"When your mother asks, 'Do you want a piece of advice?' it is a mere formality. It doesn't matter if you answer yes or no. You're going to get it, anyway."
— *Erma Bombeck*

"Did you know, when kids go to bed, you can hear yourself think again? I sound fabulous."
— *Paige Kellerman.*

"Waking your kids up for school the first day after a break is almost as much fun as birthing them was."
— *Jenny McCarthy*

"Twelve years later the memories of those nights, of that sleep deprivation, still make me rock back and forth a little bit. You want to torture someone? Hand them an adorable baby they love who doesn't sleep."
— *Shonda Rhimes*

"Mike, can't you paint on walls like other children? Do you have any idea how hard it is to get that stuff off the ceiling?" — *Michelangelo's mother*

"I love all my children equally. Except for the one that sleeps... I love that one more." — *Unknown*

"I always say if you aren't yelling at your kids, you're not spending enough time with them."
— *Reese Witherspoon*

"My mom said she learned how to swim. Someone took her out in the lake and threw her off the boat. That's how she learned how to swim. I said, 'Mom, they weren't trying to teach you how to swim.'"
— *Paula Poundstone*

"The most remarkable thing about my mother is that for 30 years she served the family nothing but leftovers. The original meal has never been found." — *Calvin Trillin*

"Usually the triumph of my day is, you know, everybody making it to the potty." — *Julia Roberts*

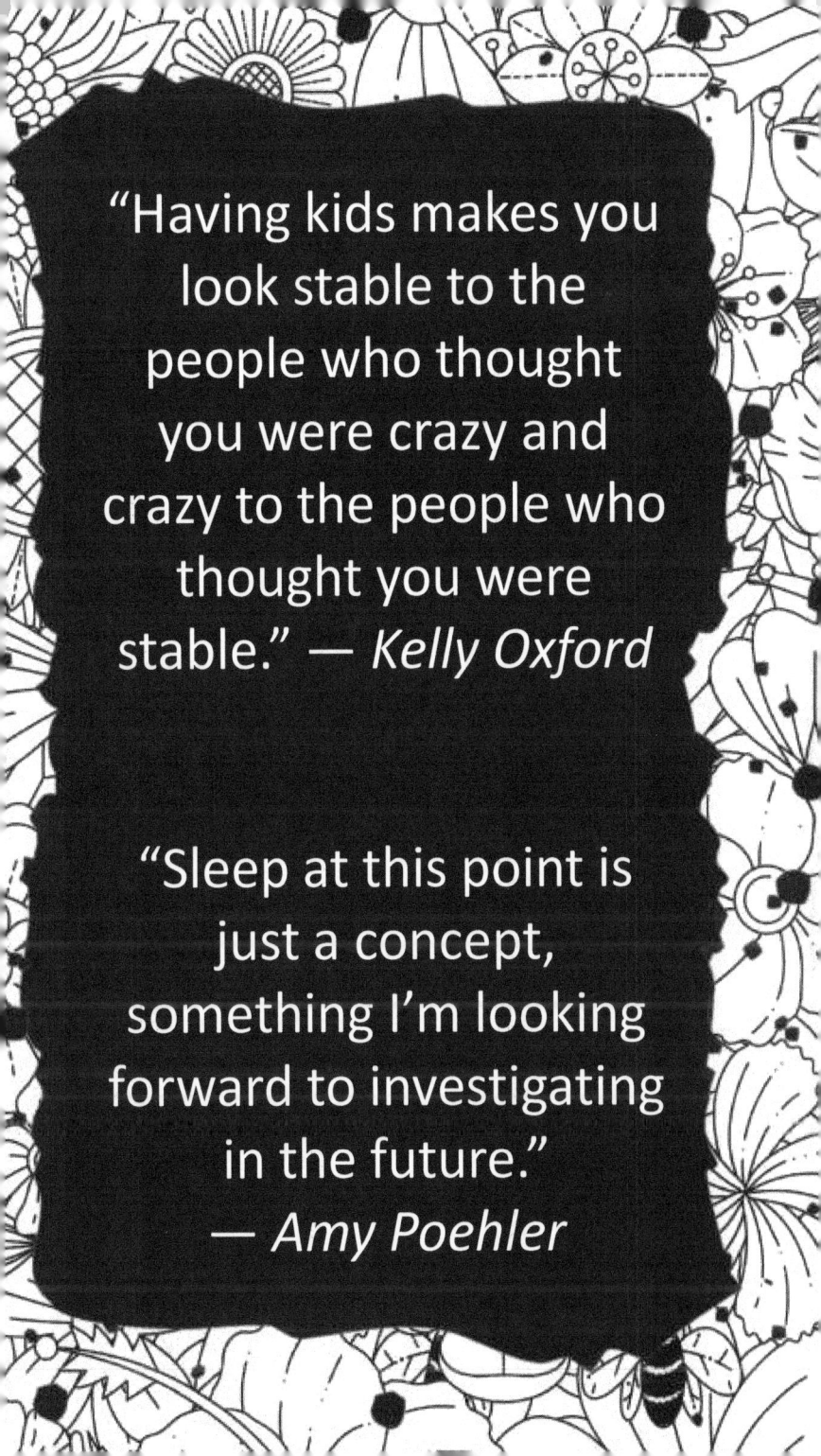

"Having kids makes you look stable to the people who thought you were crazy and crazy to the people who thought you were stable." — *Kelly Oxford*

"Sleep at this point is just a concept, something I'm looking forward to investigating in the future." — *Amy Poehler*

"It'd be cool if my kids could make something I actually want, like a bottle of wine, out of macaroni and glue."
— *Stephanie McMaster*

"Sleep at this point is just a concept, something I'm looking forward to investigating in the future." — *Amy Poehler*

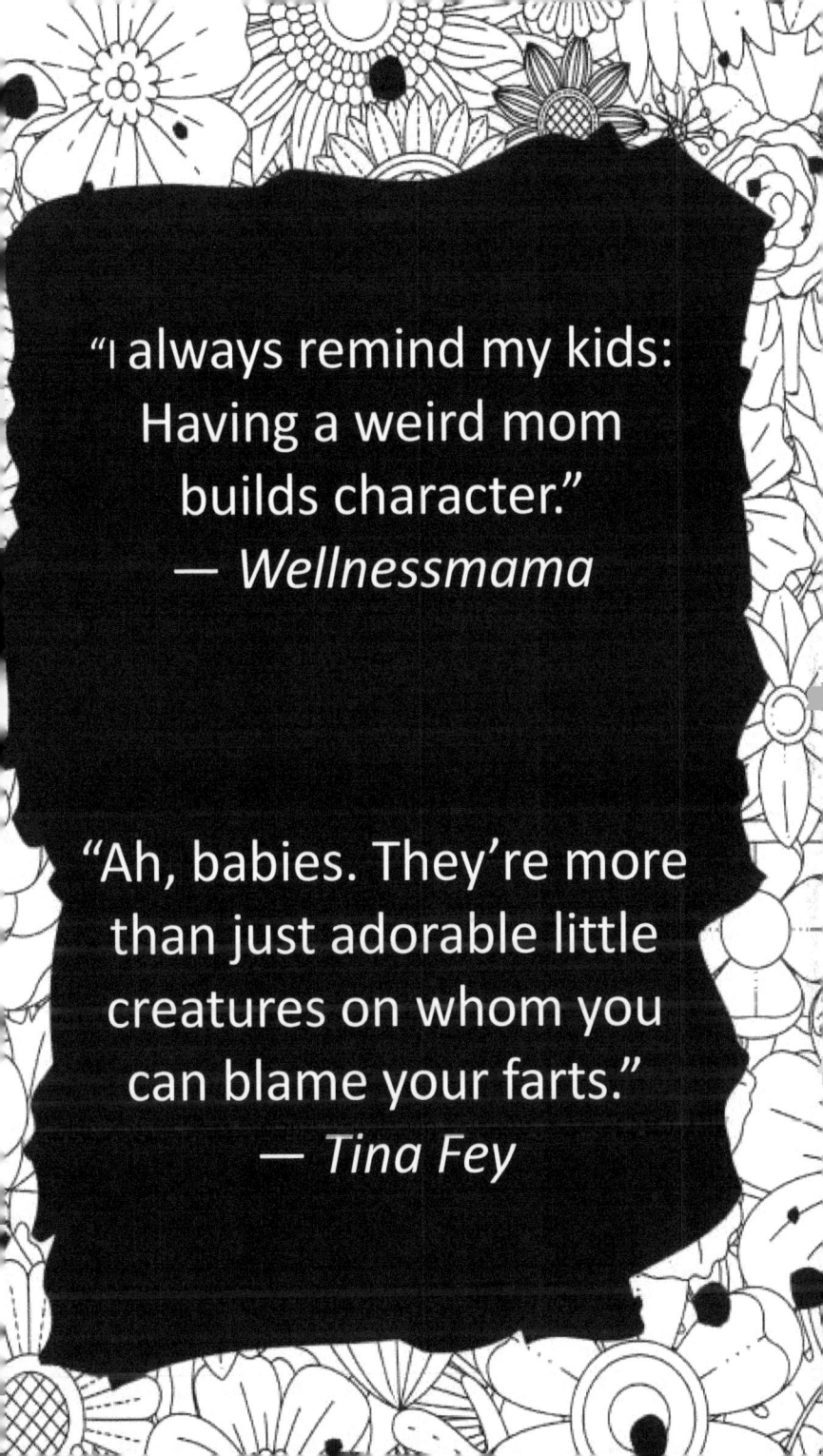

"I always remind my kids: Having a weird mom builds character."
— *Wellnessmama*

"Ah, babies. They're more than just adorable little creatures on whom you can blame your farts."
— *Tina Fey*

"My mom's favorite Stevie Wonder song is, 'I Just Called to Say Someone You Don't Know Has Cancer.'"
— *Damien Fahey*

"My kids are never better friends than when it's 30 minutes past bedtime, and they won't stop giggling."
— *The Simplified Family*

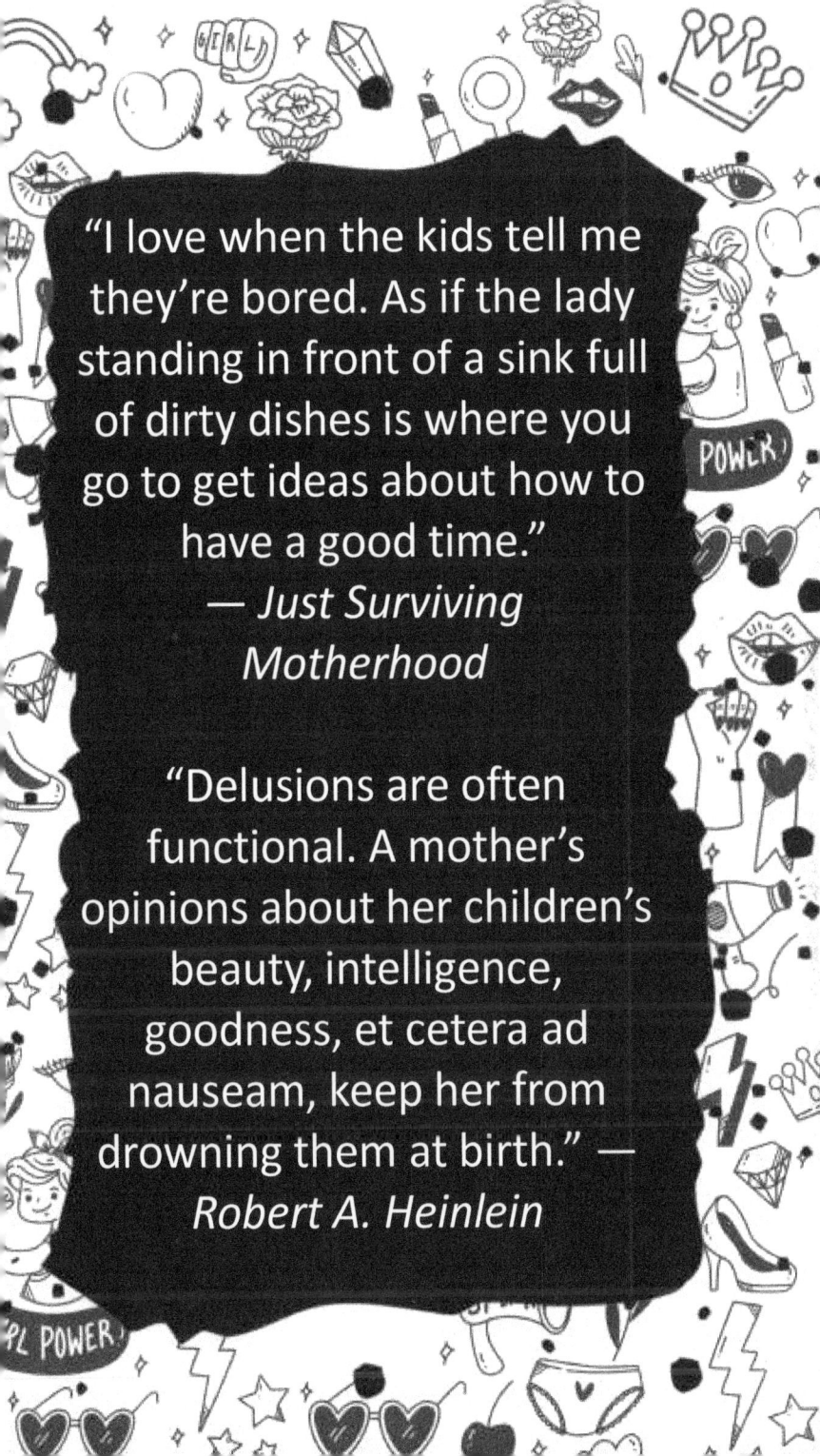

"I love when the kids tell me they're bored. As if the lady standing in front of a sink full of dirty dishes is where you go to get ideas about how to have a good time."
— *Just Surviving Motherhood*

"Delusions are often functional. A mother's opinions about her children's beauty, intelligence, goodness, et cetera ad nauseam, keep her from drowning them at birth." — *Robert A. Heinlein*

"Raising a kid is part joy and part guerilla warfare." — *Ed Asner*

"You know how once you have kids you never ever pee by yourself again? At least one of them is always in there with you at all times." — *Jennifer Garner*

"I love to play hide-and-seek with my kid, but some days my goal is to find a hiding place where he can't find me until after high school." — *Anon*

"I've conquered a lot of things... blood clots in my lungs — twice, knee and foot surgeries, winning Grand Slams being down match point, to name just a few, but I found out by far the hardest is figuring out a stroller!" — *Serena Williams*

"Children are like crazy, drunken small people in your house."
— *Julie Bowen*

"When can we come see the baby? Four a.m. would be super helpful. Thanks."
— *Just Surviving Motherhood*

"My kid is turning out to be exactly like me. Well played, Karma. Well played."
— *House Wife Plus*

Mom *Vs* Dad

To Mom: "I'm hungry, I'm tired, I'm cold, I'm hot, can I have... where are you?"
To Dad: "Where's Mom?"

"It is never easy being a mother. If it were easy, fathers would do it."

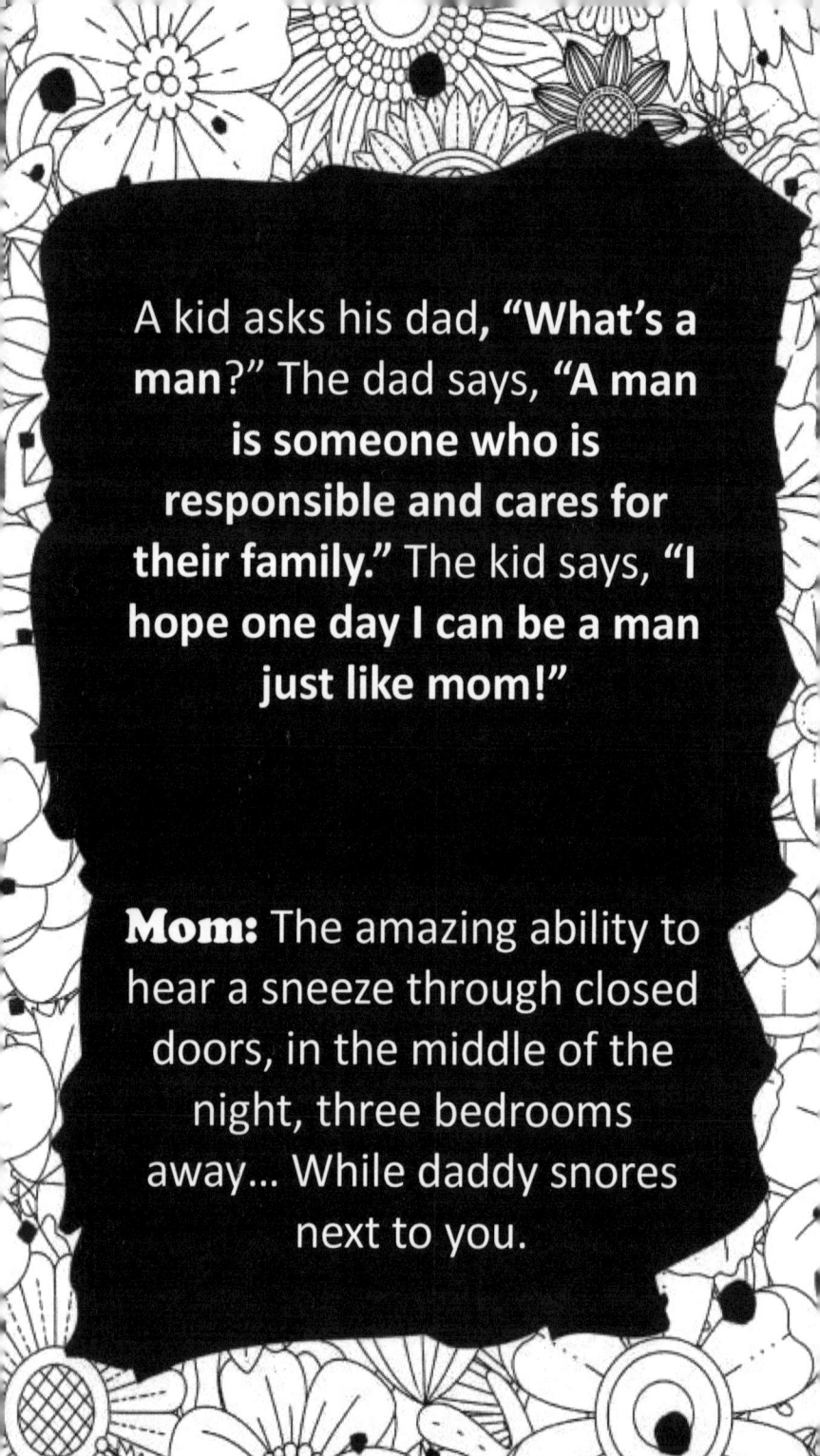

A kid asks his dad, **"What's a man?"** The dad says, **"A man is someone who is responsible and cares for their family."** The kid says, "I hope one day I can be a man just like mom!"

Mom: The amazing ability to hear a sneeze through closed doors, in the middle of the night, three bedrooms away... While daddy snores next to you.

Son: My Mom told me I'd never amount to anything because I procrastinate too much. I said, "Oh, yeah? Just you wait."

Dad: Don't wake up mom! There are at least seven species who eat their young. Your mom may be one of them.

Why is Mother's Day before Father's Day?
So the kids can spend all their Christmas money on mom.

I don't want to sleep like a baby...
I want to sleep like my husband.

Son & Mom

Son: Mom, can you give me some money?
Mom: Oh, honey, I already gave you life."

Son: "Mom, what's a weekend?"
Mom: "I don't know, sweetheart, I haven't had one since you were born."

Mother to son: "I'm warning you. If you fall out of that tree and break both your legs, don't come running to me!"

A mother said to her son, "Look at that kid over there; he's not misbehaving." The son replied, "Maybe he has good parents then!"

"Mom, are bugs good to eat?" asked the boy.
"Let's not talk about such things at the dinner table, son," his mother replied.
After dinner, the mother asked, "Now, baby, what did you want to ask me?"
"Oh, nothing," the boy said. "There was a bug in your soup, but now it's gone."

Mom No. 1: How do you get your sleepy-head son up in the morning?
Mom No. 2: I just put the cat on the bed.
Mom No. 1: How does that help?
Mom No. 2: The dogs already there.

Son: Mom, why did the chicken cross the road?
Mom: Why did you let the chicken out? Do you know how much I paid for that chicken?

What do you call a mom who isn't around much and can't seem to get their underwear into the hamper?
Dad

Son: Why is a computer so smart?

Mom: It listens to its motherboard.

Son: My mom's voice is so loud, even your neighbors brush their teeth and get dressed.

Son on Mothers Day: Don't worry about doing the dishes Mom, just relax... you can just do them in the morning."

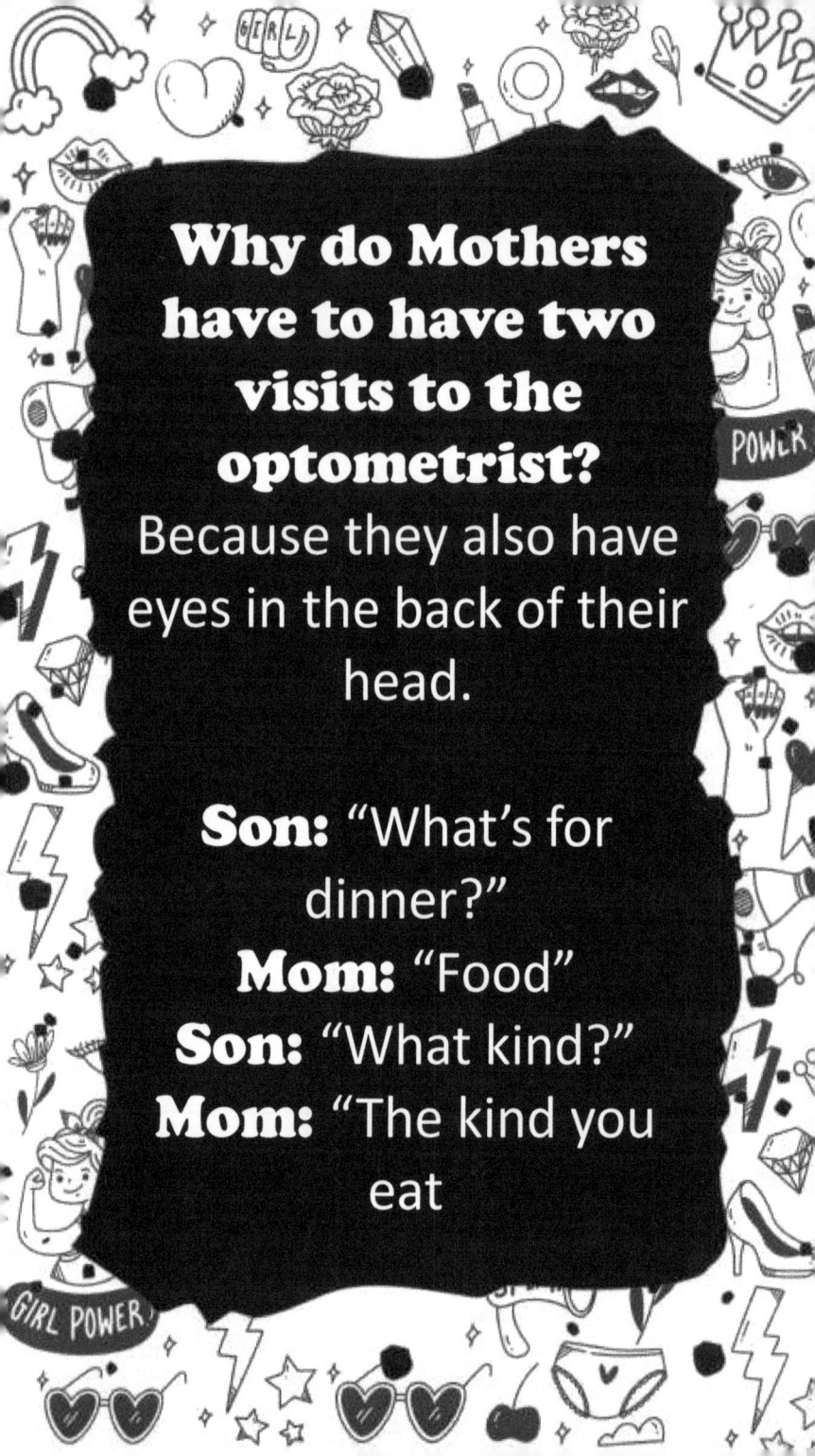

Mom: "I have the perfect son."
Friend: "Does he smoke?"
Mom: "No, he doesn't."
Friend: "Does he drink whiskey?"
Mom: "No, he doesn't."
Friend: "Does he ever come home late?"
Mom: "No, he doesn't."
Friend: "I guess you really do have the perfect son. How old is he?"
Mom: "He will be six months old next Wednesday."

Son: "When is Mother's Day, Dad?"
Dad: "Everyday son, every day."

Bought my mom a mug that says, **"Happy Mother's Day from the World's Worst Son."** I forgot to mail it, but I think she knows.

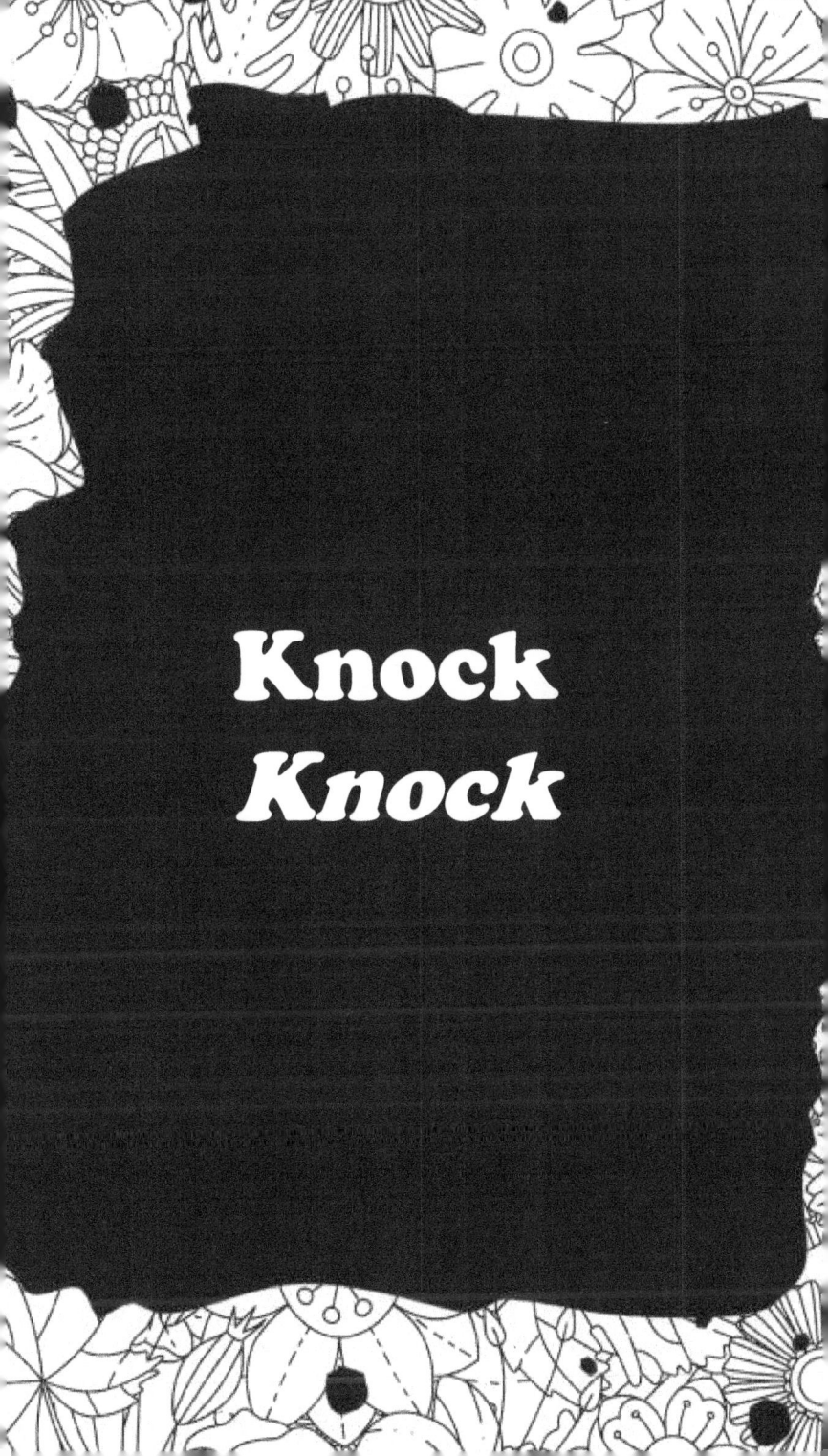

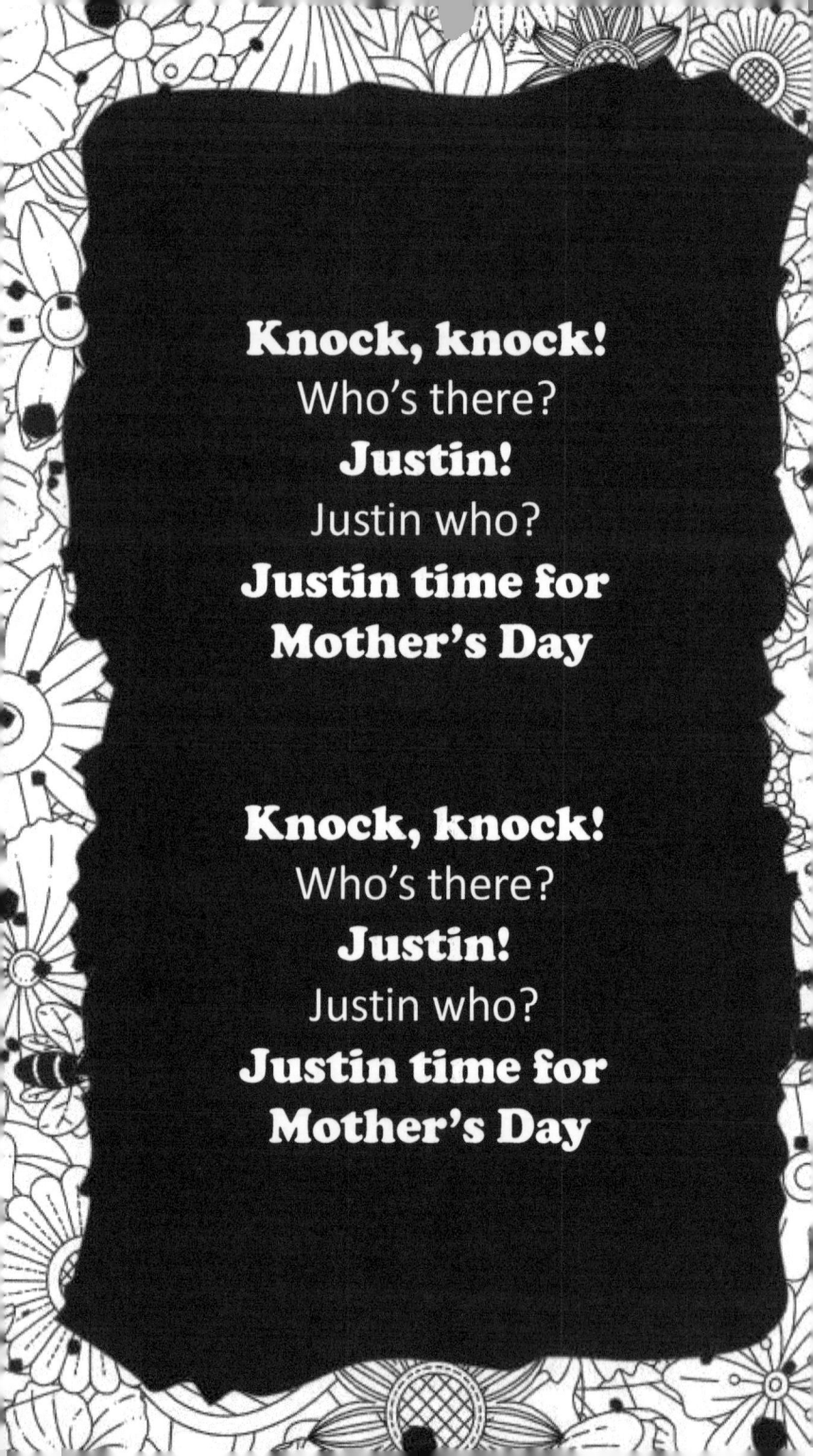

Knock, Knock.
Who's there?
Adore.
Adore who?
Adore you mommy!

Knock, knock.
Who's there?
Howard.
Howard who?
Howard you like breakfast in bed mommy?

Knock, knock
Who's there?
Annie
Annie who?
Annie thing you can do, Mum can do better.

Knock, knock.
Who's there?
Yo mama.
Yo mama who?
Yo mama who knows you didn't put out the garbage like I asked you to.

Knock, Knock.
Who's there?
Water.
Water who?
Water you doing for Mother's Day?

Knock, knock.
Who's there?
Omelet.
Omelet who?
Omelet Mommy sleep in today.

9 Things a Mom would *NEVER* say

1. How on earth can you see the TV sitting so far back?"

2. "I don't have a tissue with me... just use your sleeve."

3. "Well, if John's mamma says it's OK, that's good enough for me."

4. "Let me smell that shirt — Yeah, it's good for another week."

5. "Don't bother wearing a jacket – the wind-chill is bound to improve."

6. "Yeah, I used to skip school a lot, too."

7. "The curfew is just a general time to shoot for. It's not like I'm running a prison around here."

8. "Go ahead and keep that stray dog, honey. I'll be glad to feed and walk him every day."

9. Just leave all the lights on ... it makes the house look cheerier."

Silly *Mom* Jokes

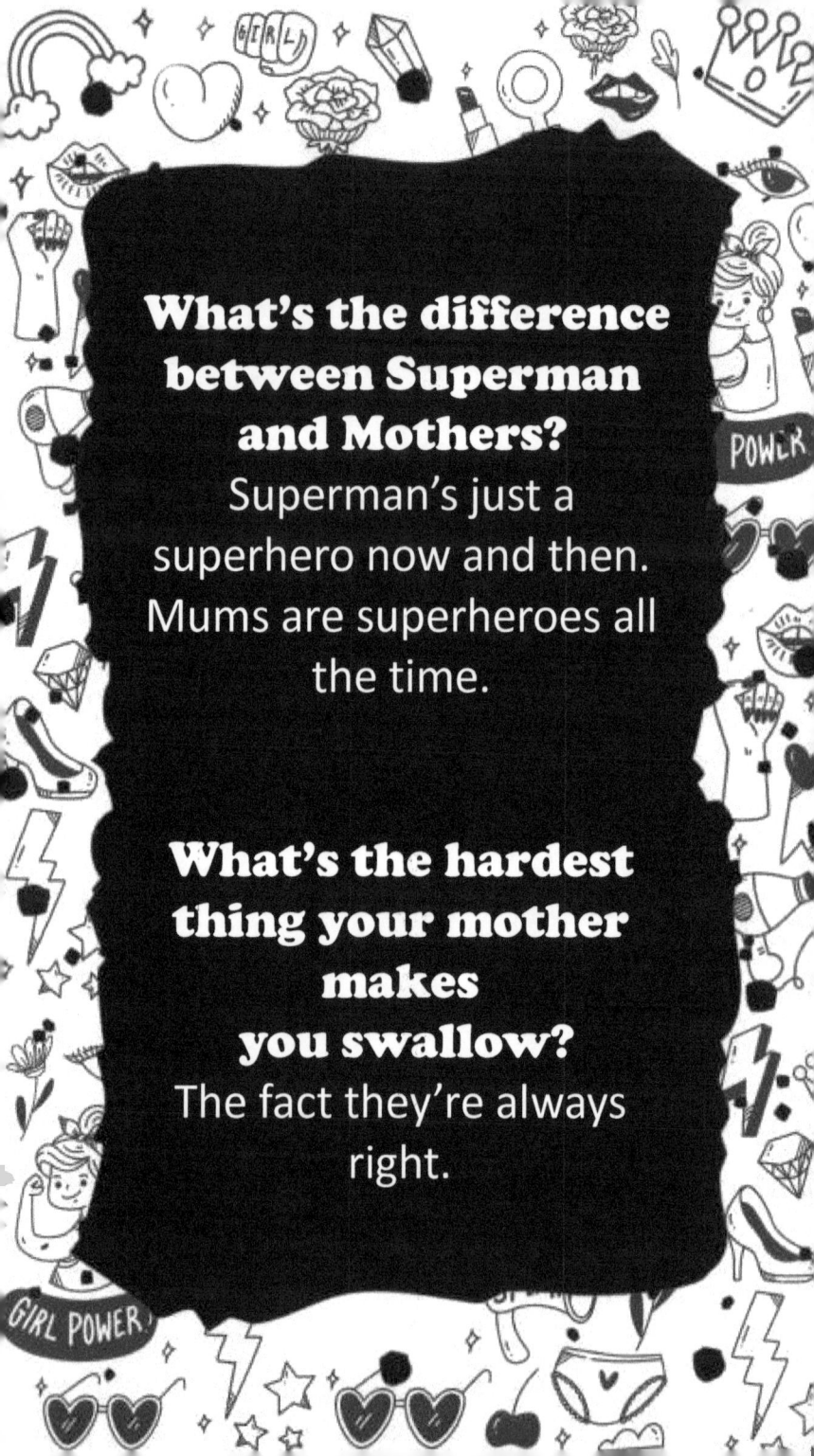

What's the difference between Superman and Mothers?
Superman's just a superhero now and then. Mums are superheroes all the time.

What's the hardest thing your mother makes you swallow?
The fact they're always right.

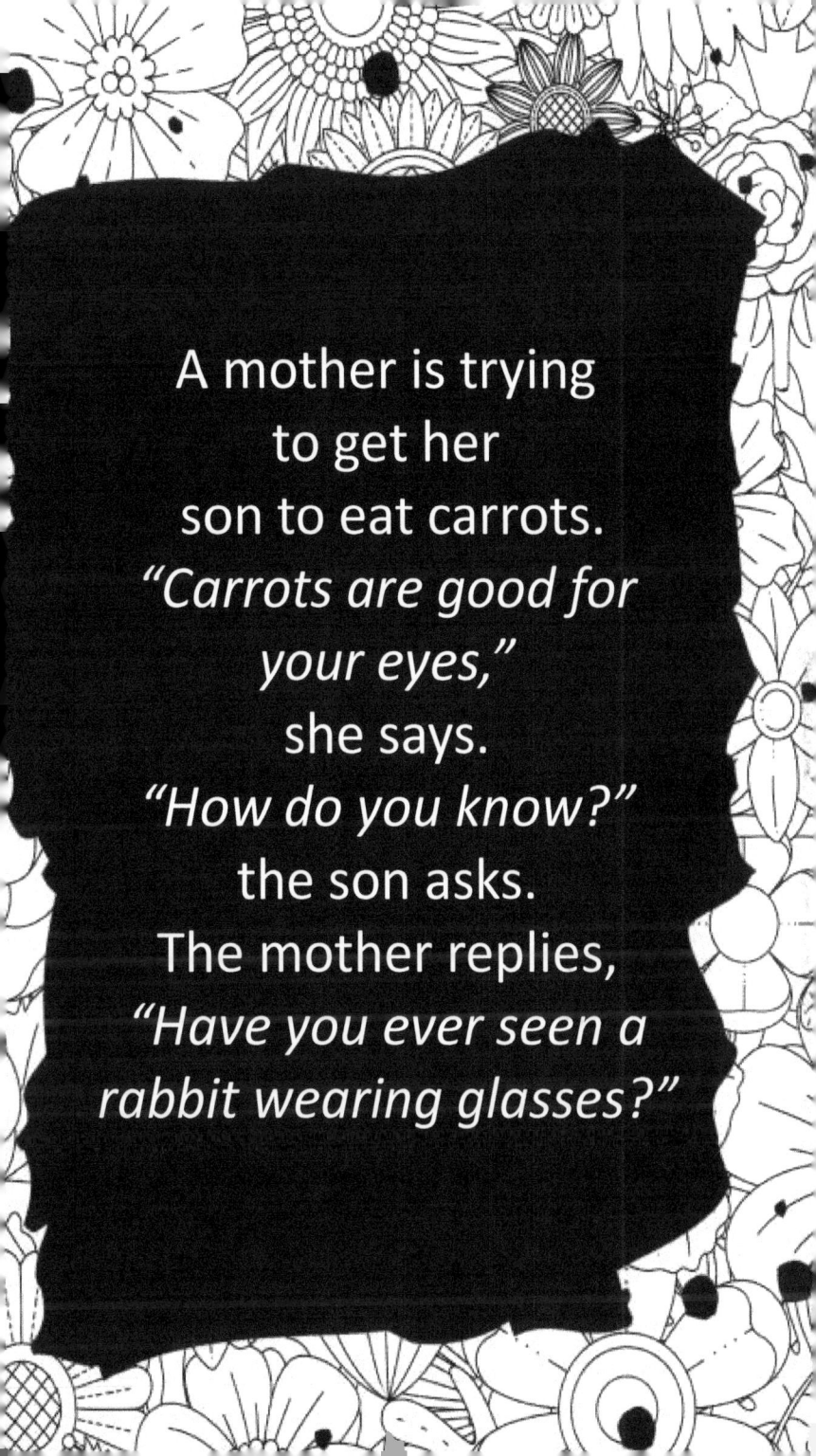

A mother is trying to get her son to eat carrots. "Carrots are good for your eyes," she says. "How do you know?" the son asks. The mother replies, "Have you ever seen a rabbit wearing glasses?"

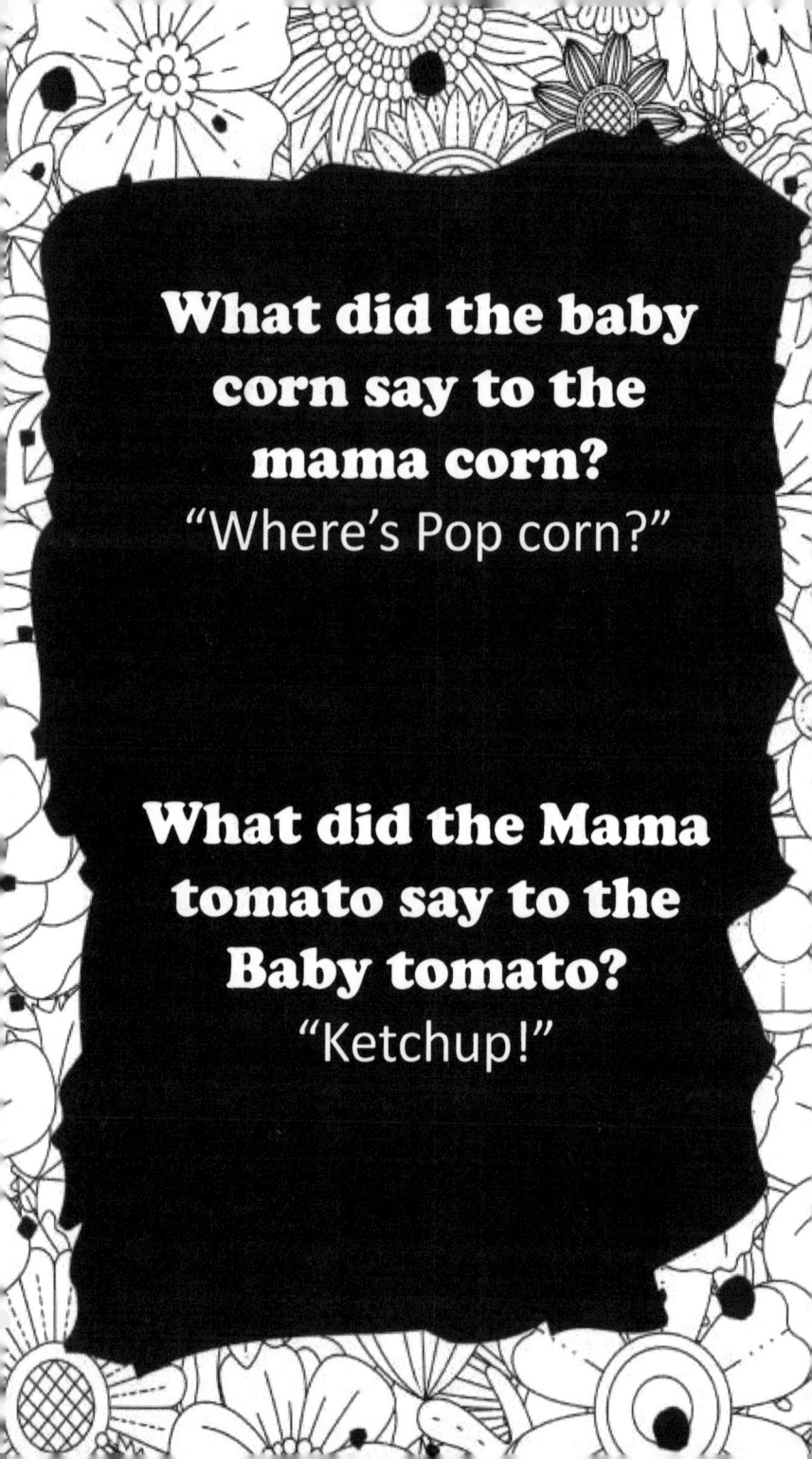

What did the baby corn say to the mama corn?
"Where's Pop corn?"

What did the Mama tomato say to the Baby tomato?
"Ketchup!"

Why did the cookie cry?

Because his mother was a wafer so long!

What do you call a small mom?

Minimum.

What makes more noise than a child jumping on mommy's bed?

Two children jumping on mommy's bed!

Yes, please get a new cup every time you need water — *said no mom ever.*

What did Mommy spider say to Baby spider?

"You spend too much time on the web."

Why did the mommy cat want to go bowling?

She was an alley cat.

Why is Mother's Day before Father's Day?
So the kids can spend all their Christmas money on Mum.

What did the mother broom say to the baby broom?
It's time to go to sweep!

How come the mother needle got mad at the baby needle?
It was way past its thread time!

How do you keep little cows quiet, so their mommy can sleep late?
Use the moooooote button.

What color flowers do mama cats like to get?
Purrrrrrrple flowers.

Roses are red,
Violets are blue.
My mom's jokes,
Are funnier than you.

Why did the baby strawberry cry?
Because his mom was in a jam!

What did the panda give his mommy?
A bear hug.

What kind of flowers are best for Mother's Day?

Moms!

Why do Mothers have to have two visits to the optometrist?

Because they also have eyes in the back of their head.

Why was it so hard for the pirate to call his mom?
Because she left the phone off the hook.

How do you get the kids to be quiet?
Say mom's the word.

What did Mommy spider say to Baby spider?
"You spend too much time on the web."

"Why did the bean children give their mom a sweater?
She was chili."

What warm drink helps mom relax?
Calm-omile tea.

Boy: "My mom is having a new baby."
Girl: "What's wrong with the old one?"

What was Cleopatra's favorite day of the year?
Mummy's day

I stubbed my toe and my Mom shouted at me for yelling, "What the duck!"
She was angry that I used fowl language.

What did the mama tomato say to the baby tomato?
Catch up!

What color flowers do mama cats like to get?
Purrrrrrple flowers.

How many moms does it take to screw in a lightbulb?

One, obviously, and she has to do it or else it won't get done.

Science teacher: *"When is the boiling point reached?"*

Student: *"When my mother sees my report card!"*

How come the mother needle got mad at the baby needle?
It was way past its thread time!

How do you keep little cows quiet, so their mommy can sleep late?
Use the moooooote button.

What did the panda give his mommy?
A bear hug.

Why don't mothers wear watches?
There's a clock on the stove.

What did the Mother broom say to the Baby broom?
"It's time to go to sweep!"

Why do Mothers have to have two visits to the optometrist?
Because they also have eyes in the back of their head.

Please excuse the mess;
my kids are making memories of me yelling at them to clean up.

Why don't they have Mother's Day sales?
Because Mothers are priceless!!!

CONCLUSION

We hope you enjoyed this collection of Mom jokes.

Creating memories with friends and family from sharing the laughter of jokes is what motivates us to create these books.

If you and your kids enjoyed this book, we would really appreciate it if you could leave a review on Amazon. It only takes a few minutes but would mean the world to us.

Don't forget to check out our website over at www.konnectdkids.com for freebies and to see the range of our great books for kids

Enjoy...

Andre Franis
Chief Joke Teller
Konnectd Kids
www.konnectdkids.com

COME AND VISIT US
www.Konnectdkids.com

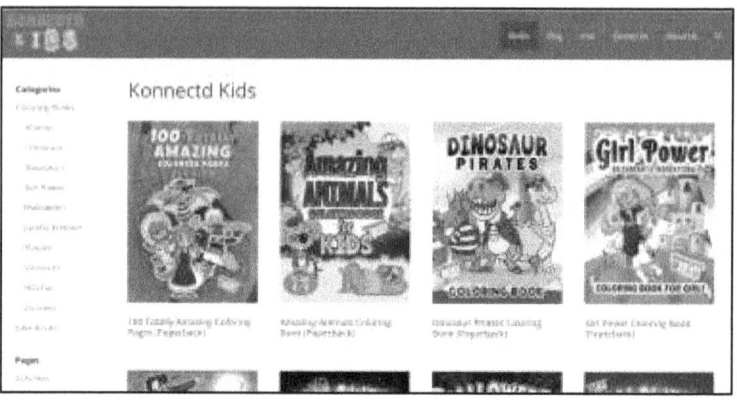

OUR PRODUCTS
www.etsy.com/shop/konnectd
konnectd.redbubble.com

OUR BOOKS
www.konnectdkids.com
www.konnectdsupply.com

FIND US ON INSTAGRAM
@Konnectdkids

FOLLOW US ON FACEBOOK
facebook.com/Konnectdkids

Come and see our range of books and resources

www.konnectdkids.com

www.ingramcontent.com/pod-product-compliance
Lightning Source LLC
Chambersburg PA
CBHW062023290426
44108CB00024B/2754